RANGER RICK'S BEST FRIENDS

HI, I'M RANGER RICK, the official conservation symbol for young members of the National Wildlife Federation, and leader of the Ranger Rick Nature Clubs. On behalf of all the animals in Deep Green Wood, welcome to our world of nature and wildlife.

The Seal Family

by Anne LaBastille

**Created and Published by
The National Wildlife Federation
Washington, D. C.**

1 The Fur Seal Rescue Squad

based on characters developed by J. A. Brownridge

The Pacific Ocean's strong winds almost took off Ranger Rick's hat as he looked out over the storm-tossed waves from a cliff near San Francisco's Golden Gate.

He smiled as he watched a group of sea lions playing in the crashing surf. While two old sea lion bulls snorted in the breeze and their cows tended the babies, a parade of youngsters jumped off into the waves. Miraculously, the diving sea lions just missed cutting them-

4

selves on the rock island's jagged edges.

Rick was glad to see that so many California sea lions were safely growing from babies to adults. Some years ago, here below San Francisco's famous Cliff House, people could see only a few of the animals. Illegal hunting and such dangers of the sea as killer whales and sharks had reduced the herd to just a few strays. "Thank goodness they're coming back in such numbers," Rick thought.

"Hey, come on!" Ollie Otter shouted to him from above. "Let's hurry or we'll be late for our trip to Yosemite National Park! I've got my mountain climber's rope and am all set to go!"

Cubby Bear leaned over the edge beside Ollie. He cupped his paw to shout against the wind. "What are all those seals down there with you, Rick?"

"They aren't seals, Cubby," Rick hollered back. "Why don't you come down and see for yourself?" Then when his friend joined him, he added, "These are the famous California sea lions. They're known for all the tricks they can learn to perform in circuses."

"What's so special about that?" Cubby asked, hanging onto the cliff. "I've got relatives in the circus too—and they can do more than just throw a ball

back and forth with their noses!"

"Well, these are remarkable animals," Rick said. "Listen to what they have to say to each other."

And as the friends leaned into the wind to catch the noise of the sea lions, they heard an unforgettable barking. "Ar-ar-ar!" the big adults said to each other.

"And listen to the little ones, too!" Ollie called. He was now clambering down the rocks to join Rick and Cubby, so interested in the sea lions that he had forgotten the mountain climbing trip to Yosemite. He pointed to a group of yearling sea lions who were yipping at each other, trying to sound just like their parents.

The friends were all watching the sea lions so attentively that they didn't notice a giant-sized wave that was roaring in from the sea. It must have come all the way from Hawaii. As it crashed against the cliff and the rock islands, gulls flew high to escape its foaming fingers.

All at once it burst upon the rock where Rick and Cubby and Ollie stood. Desperately they grabbed for firm handholds, trying to hang on with all their might. But Cubby, who stood in the most exposed position, was swept out to sea by the mighty wave. "Help!" he

called as he disappeared into the swirling depths.

Rick and Ollie looked at each other in horror. The currents of the Pacific are so strong, they feared they'd never see Cubby again. But as they peered out to sea, they saw a struggling figure not too far out. It was Cubby!

"I know what to do," Ollie said quickly. "I can use my mountain climbing rope! Here, grab one end of it." And before Rick could stop him, the agile otter plunged into the swells, with the rope streaming behind him.

Rick watched as Ollie swam his way out through the surf to their friend. Then, when Ollie signalled that the rope was secured around Cubby's waist, Rick began to pull in. Finally one very cold and very wet bear was hauled up on the rock.

Rick and Ollie tried to help get all the salt water out of Cubby's lungs. But as Cubby coughed and shivered and shook, his friends realized that he was trying to say something important.

"There's a little seal out there," Cubby blubbered. "Just a little one... probably a baby."

"Where?" Rick asked, shielding his eyes against the blast of the wind.

"I think I see him," Ollie cried, pointing beyond the rocks. It was just a tiny black speck, tossed about by the foaming waters.

"Yes!" Rick answered. "I think it may be a fur seal."

"I don't care what kind of a seal it is," Ollie said. "Or even if it's a walrus or a sea lion. We've got to do what we can to

save it—if it's still alive."

"You're right, Ollie," Rick agreed. "Let's try to form the Fur Seal Rescue Squad. Do you think you can make it out there once more?"

"I'll sure give it a try, Rick," Ollie declared. Then into the waves he dove again. Cubby and Rick watched him swim with all his strength. Finally he reached the baby seal, looped his rope around it, and signalled to his friends.

Like a trained team of Coast Guardsmen, Rick and Cubby pulled in on the line, hand over hand. Even as the wind blew harder and the waves crashed around them, they kept pulling.

When the little seal at last lay at their feet on the rock, it was barely able to breathe. Battered and exhausted, it limply flapped its flippers.

"The ocean sure is rough in this part of the country," Cubby said as they lifted the baby fur seal to safety. "But why do seals have trouble in the water—they live there just like fish, don't they?"

"Yes, but they're mammals," Rick explained. "They need to breathe air just like we have to, Cubby. And although they're born able to swim, they're pretty defenseless in the big, dangerous sea. Sometimes their mothers disappear, too. So there's no one to feed them if they're still at the nursing stage."

"Gosh!" Ollie said. "We'd better get this seal to a first-aid station fast. It may be starving to death!"

"That's right," Rick said. "Lots of us don't think how hard life is for our close relatives who live in the sea. The long distances they have to swim, and the difficulties along the way, mean that only a fraction of them survive. Maybe if our Ranger friends read this book, they'll learn more about sea mammals and will want to help keep track of them. But of course, not all Rangers will be so brave and well equipped as Ollie was!"

"That reminds me," Ollie said. "Who wants to go mountain climbing?"

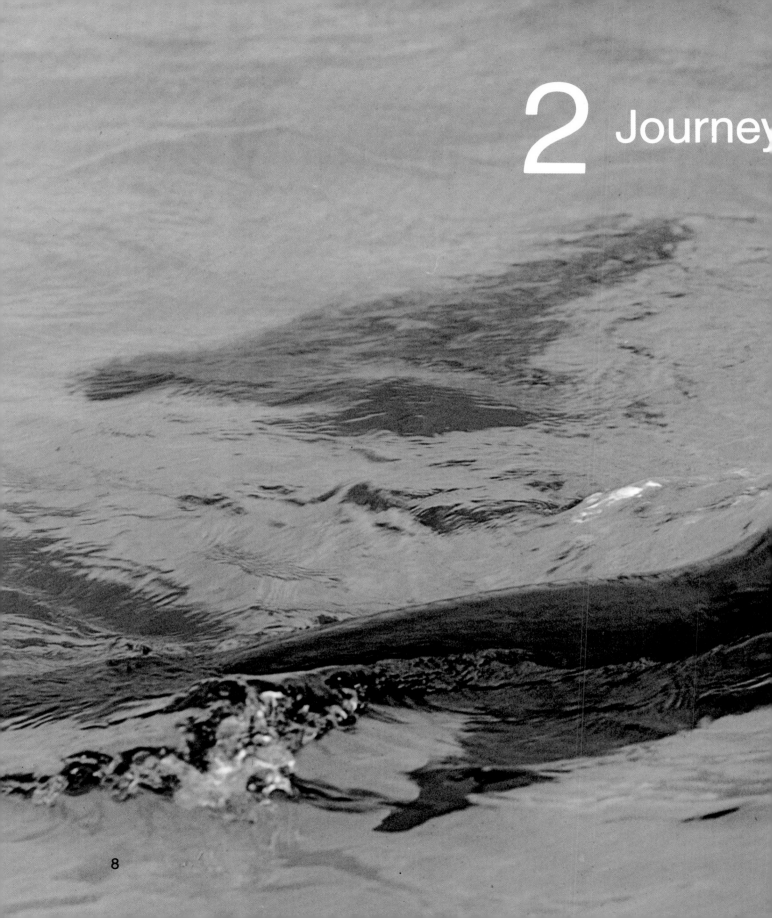

Sonya swam slowly through the sea. The California spring sunshine felt warm on her rich brown fur. She flipped her short tail and turned a somersault restlessly. Just as in years past, it was time to swim north again to the land where she had been born five years before.

Mothers of some of Sonya's friends swam past; they were already beginning the long journey. They were heading for the Pribilofs (PRIB-a-loffs) and other small islands between Alaska and Russia, 3,000 miles away.

At the same time that Sonya and her friends began heading north to their summer home, other fur seals along the west coast of the United States and from Japan were also moving toward the Pribilofs. But only females and pups were making the long trek. Older males had spent the winter in the north, near the Alaskan coast. In early May they would return to the islands to meet Sonya and the others.

By day Sonya swam at about seven miles per hour, easily keeping pace with the rest. By night she

Paddling with front flippers, a fur seal surges northward.

9

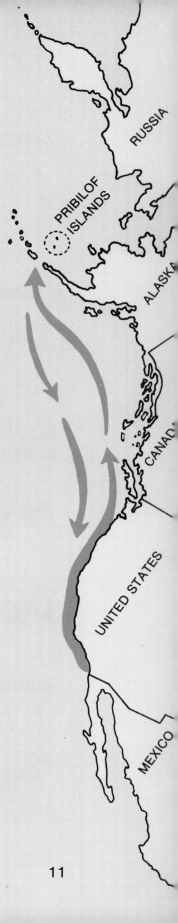

Cows and pups are guarded by bulls (left) at the end of their long journey.

rested, floating sometimes on her back, sometimes on her side.

Sonya saw none of the killer whales or sharp-toothed sharks which are the seal's enemies. But before the trip was over, some of her friends were gone.

It was the end of June when Sonya finally reached the Pribilof Islands with land to rest on and a well-stocked sea to eat in.

Already there were a million and a half fur seals crowding the beaches, and more to come. Sonya felt a wave of excitement.

All along the rocky beach Sonya saw huge males, 600 pounds or more, sitting proudly. Their necks were swollen. Muscles bulged under the sleek, blackish fur.

Would one of them want Sonya for his mate, the way he had last year? She scrambled out of the water and looked around. A beach-master, a bull who had claimed his share of the rookery early in May, waddled toward her. Proud and strong, he pushed her into a group

11

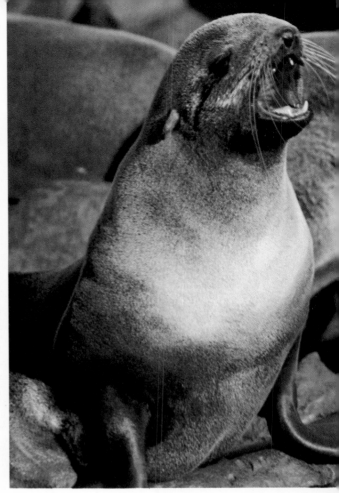

A brand-new fur seal slumbers . . . as mother bawls triumphantly.

of female seals. She would be another of his "wives."

Sonya stayed in the rookery with the bull and the noisy throng of other cows and seal pups. But she felt strange and different. Something special was about to happen.

Two days later she gave birth to her first pup, a baby that had been growing inside her since the summer before. Most of the other female seals gave birth too; a new pup was being born every five seconds.

Sonya was happy, though she saw that her little one looked like all the others—black, two feet long, and about twelve pounds. He sounded like all the others, too—hungry.

But Sonya knew which was hers. She named him Serge, and she fed him lots of milk, the richest milk any mother can offer. It was so rich (fifty percent fat) that after two weeks Sonya could leave her pup alone and go off to eat and rest. Serge would stay warm and contented for a week or more.

When Sonya came back, Serge was crying. So were thousands of other babies. But Serge's mother found him on that island, even among all those other look-alikes!

Serge grew fast. His black fur lightened to a soft gray. He learned to swim and dive. At two months he could go alone into the sea to catch squid, anchovies, and herring. But he stayed in shallow water. At four months he joined other pups in a "pod," a group of seals that would

This one's mine! Back from dinner, mother easily claims her own pup.

keep each other company in the water and on the land. This was his nursery. Here he stayed while his mother was at the rookery.

In early fall the beachmasters left the islands. The mating season was over and they were tired and hun-gry. Most had not eaten for two or three months because they had been afraid to leave their territory.

Just before winter set in, Sonya started for California once more, followed by little Serge. But he would not go all the way. Summers

14

he would swim to the Pribilofs, but he would not live on the rookery. That was for cows and pups and grown males. He would stay with the other young bulls farther inland.

Hunters would catch some of Serge's friends, three and four year old seals. The law said they could. But Serge would be one of the young bulls left to breed with the females.

When he was nine or ten he would become a beachmaster, too. He would rule his own part of the great seal rookery.

3 The Fin-Footed Family

Sonya has many seal relatives around the world. They all belong to a group called *pinnipeds* (PIN-a-peds), or "fin-feet." All are wonderful swimmers. With fin-shaped feet and streamlined bodies they move easily through the water. They also have eyes that see better under water than on land.

Sonya and other fur seals are called eared seals (see page 30). Unlike other seals they have ear flaps, not just holes in the sides of their heads. There are other differences. On land, eared seals can turn their rear flippers forward to walk about—something earless seals can't do.

California sea lions are eared seals, too. They are the kind of seals you see doing tricks in a circus.

The harp seal off the coast of Maine is an earless seal, and so its rear flippers trail behind like a fish tail. The harp seal's coat is whitish or silvery in color, with black, harp-shaped marks.

The young, covered with snowy-white fur, are the prettiest of all fin-foots. But they get a sudden shock when born: from their mothers' warm bodies they come right out onto a frozen bed of ice!

The babies drink as much milk as possible to build blubber. They may gain 50 pounds in two weeks. Then their mothers begin to leave them alone. The pups must live off their own fat until they are brave enough to enter the sea. In the water, harp seals

Sea lions sport playfully (left). On the ice (right) a newborn harp seal hides shyly.

can find fish and survive.

Most pinnipeds live in cold water. Weddell seals, part of the earless branch of the family, live in Antarctic waters around firm ice. In fact, they spend a lot of time *under* the ice in winter.

How do they breath? By finding little domes in the ice where air is trapped or by biting holes with their teeth.

Their close neighbor, the fierce leopard seal, has sharp teeth, too. He uses them to attack smaller seals and sea birds, including penguins.

Largest of all pinnipeds is the elephant seal, a strange-looking fellow

(see next page). The male has a long nose, like an elephant's trunk. When he's calm, it's wrinkled up and short. When he's angry, it's puffed out.

Walruses (see page 21) make up the third family in the fin-foot group. They are almost as big as the elephant seals. Some males grow to 3,000 pounds—about the weight of your family car!

Note the tusks. These are the special trademark that makes them different from all other pinnipeds.

Turn the pages if you want to read a walrus adventure.

Although male Weddell seals "sing", mother seals and their pups call to each other with a bawling "Wa-a-a-a".

Immense size makes elephant seals (left) and the walrus (below) fearless.

4 Ookuk The Brave

Ookuk was hungry. The five-year old walrus dove down to the sea's floor. There he felt along the sand with his tough whiskers, finding clams and sucking in the delicious meat. Again and again he dove.

His hunger eased, Ookuk swam slowly to an ice floe crowded with walruses. He caught hold with tusk and flipper, and hauled himself aboard. The pale arctic sun shone down on his rust-brown hide.

Peering across the water, Ookuk could see Pudlo, the littlest of the herd, riding through the water on his mother's back. Pudlo's mother settled him down on a nearby chunk of ice. Then she went off to hunt for her share of the clams, snails, and shrimps that walruses like. The mischievous Pudlo soon slipped into the water, hurrying off on his own adventure.

Meanwhile another big walrus

Walruses, fat with blubber, huddle happily on slabs of ice.

23

Walrus warriors (right) charge to the rescue of a floundering calf (above).

clambered up beside Ookuk. It was one walrus too many! The ice floe, overburdened with tons of walrus, broke, and Ookuk slid into the sea. When he bobbed to the surface, Ookuk scanned the water to be sure everyone was all right. Suddenly he realized that Pudlo was nowhere in sight.

Then Ookuk heard a cry of OOK-OOK-OOK, thin and high-pitched. Louder it came, and more frantic. It was Pudlo, calling for help.

In the distance Ookuk spied the five-foot fin of a killer whale rising like a knife out of the water. Without thinking of safety, Ookuk sped toward the black and white monster.

The whale had already begun to attack Pudlo. It reared high in the air, opening and closing its jaws.

Before other whales might join the attack, Ookuk charged between the killer and Pudlo. The whale's cone-shaped teeth tore into Ookuk, but the walrus refused to retreat. Just then, a squad of other bellowing walruses arrived to help fight, while Pudlo crawled to a safe position on Ookuk's back.

Ookuk hurried off carrying little Pudlo out of danger. Within minutes, the little walrus' terrified mother claimed him.

Pudlo snuggled up beside her on the ice, happy but a little hungry.

5 SOS for the Whitecoats

based on characters developed by J. A. Brownridge

"Ahoy, mate," shouted Ollie Otter cheerfully as Ranger Rick stepped out from the cabin onto the deck of the big fishing boat.

Rick and his friends Ollie Otter and Sammy Squirrel had set sail from the Penobscot River in Maine to look for seals in Canada. Now, after a few days of sailing in a northeasterly direction toward Canada, their ship was in the storm-tossed Gulf of St. Lawrence. Here the mighty St. Lawrence River joins the Atlantic Ocean.

"This is where we're supposed to carry out our seal assignment," Rick told the others. "There are some seals up here the government's worried about—the harp seals. And we're supposed to find out about them."

"How could the beautiful harp seals be in any trouble?" Ollie asked. "No one would want to hurt one of them—they look just like cute little balls of fluff!"

"That's a part of the problem," Rick answered. "The harp seals have such pure white fur when they're young that people want to make coats out of them."

"You mean the sealers only go after the young?" Sammy asked, surprised at what he was hearing.

"No," Rick replied, "They harvest older ones, but they like the young seals' fur best. Harp seals are called 'whitecoats' when they're just a few days old and still nursing. Later they moult and grow different fur; then they start moving around and swimming on their own. By then they're maybe a month old—no longer white but still valuable for their hides and their oil, just like other bigger seals."

"I guess the people up here have always hunted seals and whales, haven't they, Rick?" Sammy asked. "They need the hides and the food."

"That's right," Rick answered. "But recently the hunting's increased. Not many years ago, hunters were taking as many as 200,000 harp seals a year from the ice floes in Canada. So the International Commision for the Northwest Atlantic Fisheries has set up guidelines to control the hunting. Now the Canadian government and others have laws about how many harp seals can be taken and when."

"You mean just like managing the wildlife in our Deep Green Wood?" Sammy asked.

"Yes, just like our hunting season," Rick nodded. "Here they've limited the hunting season to a short period so the harp seal herd will be allowed to remain healthy. They want to be sure that sealers of all nations obey the laws."

"Why does there have to be any hunting at all, Rick?" Sammy asked.

"Some scientists say that if no harvesting was allowed, there'd be too many harp seals for the territory," Rick explained. "There are about two million of the seals now, and there might be as many as four million if they were allowed to multiply without control. Then lots of them would starve and die of sickness, and all of them would suffer."

"Hey! The ship's turned," Ollie noticed. "The rocking and rolling feels different. We must be getting nearer the Newfoundland seal pack. Look out!"

But before Rick and Sammy heard him, they were knocked off their feet by a huge wave that came crashing over the ship's rail.

"Hah, hah! Ahoy there, ye land-lubbers!" called a strange voice.

Rick and his friends looked up in surprise. Then they looked at each other, wondering who was laughing at them. Finally they looked through the porthole of the ship's wheelhouse. And there on the captain's shoulder they saw a parrot with black eyes and a big yellow beak. "Hah, hah! Ahoy there, ye landlubbers!" it said again.

They all hurried into the wheelhouse to say hello. The captain introduced Rick, Sammy, and Ollie to the parrot, whose name was Polly.

"What else can she say besides 'Ahoy?' " Rick asked.

"She often says 'Look out for the iceberg!' " the captain answered. "She knows that scares sailors; she laughs when they look around to see the iceberg that's going to crash into their ship!"

But then suddenly he turned away to listen to the radio which had begun to crackle behind him. He listened carefully to the message.

"Wonder what's the matter?" Ollie softly asked Rick.

"It's something about seals," Rick said, trying to listen to the radio, too. "The season for hunting harp seals has ended, but some ships are slow in leaving the territory."

"Gosh!" Sammy said, "I wonder how we can help."

As they tried to think of what they might do, the ship continued north along the coast of Newfoundland through the strait that leads to the Labrador Sea. As if by magic, the rough and foggy weather cleared, and they entered a bright and glistening sea. Even though he was worried about the harp seals, Rick felt better when he saw the beautiful icy scene.

Suddenly Rick had an idea. "Can you send messages to the other ships on your radio?" he asked the captain.

"Yes, I can transmit," the captain answered. "We also have an emergency sending band on which we can send SOS calls if there's an emergency."

"Well, could you reach those ships that aren't obeying the law?"

"Sure, Rick. But there's nothing I could say that would make them go away. There are already inspectors on board who must be telling them to leave."

"Let's see what Polly thinks about this," Rick declared. "What do you say about ice, Polly?" he asked, picking up the microphone.

"Look out for the iceberg! Look out for the iceberg!" Polly squawked.

"Do it again, Rick," Sammy called from the ship's deck. "I think I see some action."

Rick held the microphone even closer to Polly's beak. "Look out for the iceberg!"

"There they go!" Sammy cried. Ollie and Rick looked out to where he was pointing. They saw three distant ships disappearing over the white horizon.

"Iceberg is a word they don't like to hear, no matter who says it," Ollie chuckled.

"Yes," the captain agreed. "That takes care of that."

"I wish it did," Rick said with a frown. "But I'm afraid that the problem of enforcing laws on the seas remains just as big as ever. What we need is a world-wide Coast Guard, maybe helped by a group of specially trained Rangers, to look after marine wildlife."

"Ahoy!" Polly said, as if she agreed.

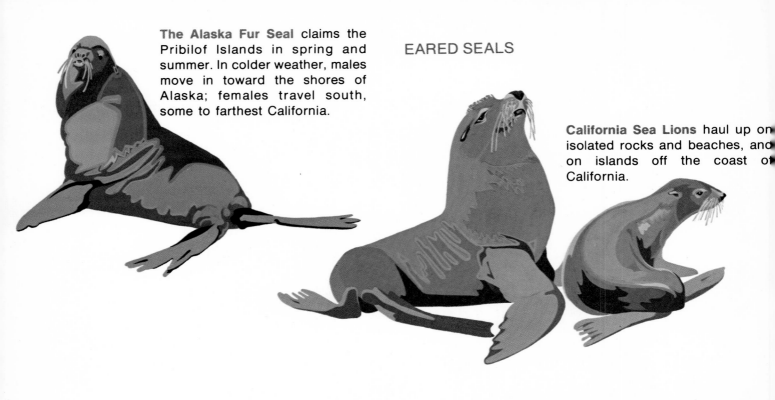

The **Alaska Fur Seal** claims the Pribilof Islands in spring and summer. In colder weather, males move in toward the shores of Alaska; females travel south, some to farthest California.

EARED SEALS

California Sea Lions haul up on isolated rocks and beaches, and on islands off the coast of California.

EARLESS SEALS

The **Leopard Seal**, loner and villain of the pinniped family, wanders Antarctic waters north to Australia, New Zealand, and South America.

The **Elephant Seal** of the north shares California islands with his pinniped cousins. The southern elephant seal inhabits the frozen shores of Antarctica.

Harp Seals summer in the Arctic. In late winter and early spring they can be found in the Gulf of St. Lawrence and off the coast of Labrador.

30

WHERE SEALS LIVE

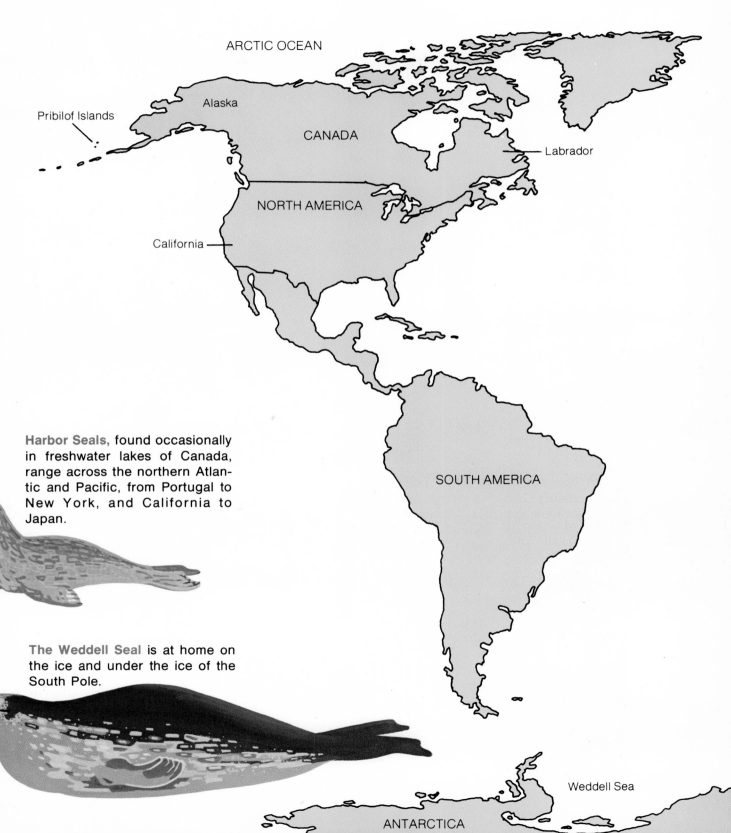

NORTH POLE

ARCTIC OCEAN

Pribilof Islands

Alaska

CANADA

NORTH AMERICA

Labrador

California

SOUTH AMERICA

Harbor Seals, found occasionally in freshwater lakes of Canada, range across the northern Atlantic and Pacific, from Portugal to New York, and California to Japan.

The Weddell Seal is at home on the ice and under the ice of the South Pole.

Weddell Sea

ANTARCTICA

WHEN YOU SEE A SEAL...

You will be delighted by the big whiskers and friendly face.

But what kind of a seal is it? Look the animal over carefully, and you will be able to tell at once. Tightly wrapped little scrolls on either side of his head say that the sea lion pictured above is an eared seal.

Check his flippers, too. The Alaska fur seal has big, bare ones that are good for swimming and cooling. They don't hold the heat the way the rest of his heavily furred body does.

The earless seal will appear to have no ears at all, just tiny holes. His limbs are also quite different— look at the furry hind flippers of the harbor seal directly above. They can't be bent forward to help walking on land.

But the most remarkable thing about seals is that they're mammals. Would you ever see a fish nursing like the happy baby seal above?

CREDITS

Robert W. Stevens cover, Alaska fur seal family; Barbara C. Peterson 2-3, Weddell seals; Bruce Coleman Inc. 8-9; Fred Bruemmer 10-11, 12 (top right), 13; Steve McCutcheon 12 (top left), 15, 24; Terry Wilson 14; George Harrison 16; Dr. Lars Karstad 17; Carleton Ray 18-19, 32 (left); Bob Evans 20; Leonard Lee Rue III 21; Joe Rychetnik 22-23, 25; Jeff Foott 32 (right); Robert Dunne back cover, red-eared turtle. Drawings pp. 30-31 by Frank Fretz.

Ranger Rick Adventures—based on characters developed by J. A. Brownridge.

The Editors are grateful for text and picture assistance provided by the staffs of the Federation's Membership Publications—NATIONAL WILDLIFE MAGAZINE, INTERNATIONAL WILDLIFE MAGAZINE, and RANGER RICK'S NATURE MAGAZINE.

NATIONAL WILDLIFE FEDERATION

Thomas L. Kimball	*Executive Vice President*
J. A. Brownridge	*Administrative Vice President*
James Davis	*Book Development*

Staff for This Book

EDITOR	Russell Bourne
ASSOCIATE EDITOR	Natalie S. Rifkin
ART DIRECTOR	Ellen Robling
RANGER RICK ART	Lorin Thompson
EDITORIAL ASSISTANT	Nancy Faries
PRODUCTION AND PRINTING	Mel M. Baughman, Jr.
CONSULTANT	Edwin Gould, Ph.D.
	The Johns Hopkins University

OUR OBJECTIVES

To encourage the intelligent management of the life-sustaining resources of the earth—its productive soil, its essential water sources, its protective forests and plantlife, and its dependent wildlife—and to promote and encourage the knowledge and appreciation of these resources, their interrelationship and wise use, without which there can be little hope for a continuing abundant life.